M000268444

Ms. Whisk's Kindergarten Magic through Food:

EGYPT

Ms. Whisk's Kindergarten Magic through Food:

EGYPT

ANN GORMAN

MILL CITY PRESS

Mill City Press, Inc.
2301 Lucien Way #415
Maitland, FL 32751
407.339.4217
www.millcitypress.net

© 2018 by Ann Gorman

Illustrator: Molly McGreevy

All rights reserved solely by the author. The author guarantees all contents are original and do not infringe
upon the legal rights of any other person or work. No part of this book may be reproduced in any form without
the permission of the author. The views expressed in this book are not necessarily those of the publisher.

Printed in the United States of America.

ISBN-13: 9781545626887

DEDICATION PAGE

As a kindergarten teacher and someone who loves to cook, I want to dedicate this book to my husband and three children, who have supported me through this journey. It has been a long time coming, and I am so excited to see what comes of this journey. I would also like to dedicate this book to the many kindergarten children who have gone through my doors over the last twelve years. I enjoyed the cooking experience with each of you. You also inspired me to write it down, to show the world. Lastly, I dedicate this to my father whom I can feel in my heart each day, his gentle touch (nudge) from above on my shoulder letting me know that I can write.

BOOK SUMMARY

The lovable character of Ms. Whisk, along with her kindergarten class, creates magic through food. While the children are creating a recipe, the room magically changes into that country. This magic sparks questions about the country. This excitement makes Ms. Whisk very happy, and she knows they are ready to learn.

Once upon a time there was a kindergarten teacher who loooved to cook. She was a magician of sorts with cooking. Her name was Ms. Whisk. The only way she could do magic was with her kindergarten class.

Ms. Whisk wanted to travel the world, so she asked her kindergarten class, "Will you cook with me?"

The children, of course, said, "Yes, we would love to!"

This was what Ms. Whisk wanted to hear. She knew now that her travels and magic would begin.

Ms. Whisk was so excited that they wanted to cook with her that she went to her closet and brought out aprons and hats for each of them. She said, "These are the clothes that will help us to create magic."

All the children smiled and couldn't wait to get started.

Ms. Whisk told the children, "We are going to be cooking around the world. It will be magical. We will travel the world with our imagination and learn a lot about where the foods come from in each country. Are you ready to explore?"

The children with excitement in their voices said, "When do we start?"

"Right now!"

"Where will we go first, and what will we make?" they called out.

"We are going to travel to Egypt," Ms. Whisk said.

"Wow! That sounds like fun! What kind of food do they have there?"

"They eat many different kinds of foods: beans, vegetables, fish, lamb, poultry and fruits. We are going to make a recipe called baklava. This is an Egyptian dessert."

The children laughed. "Baklava is a funny name!"

Ms. Whisk agreed and laughed with them.

"So, who would like to learn how to make this dessert?"

All the children chimed in, "We would!" and waved their arms in the air with excitement.

"OK, then first we need to wash our hands and put on our aprons and hats if we want any magic to happen."

The children scurried around the room washing their hands and putting on their aprons and hats.

Once they were ready, they came to the table that Ms. Whisk had set up for everyone to gather around. There on the table were all the ingredients to make the baklava.

Ms. Whisk said, "Take a few deep breaths so you can find the calm place in your bodies. This will help us when we start to put all our ingredients together. Ingredients are sensitive and like it when everyone is paying attention to them."

Ms. Whisk asked, "Who's ready to create a yummy dessert?"

"We are!" said the children in eager voices.

"OK, then let's get cooking!"

Ms. Whisk put the children in groups. Some of the children added coconut, walnuts and butter in a bowl and mixed it with a spoon. Others unrolled the phyllo dough to make it flat. Another group sprayed the phyllo dough with butter-flavored cooking spray as it was laid out on the cutting board.

Finally, Ms. Whisk put the nut mixture along the edge of the phyllo and then rolled it into a log and cut it into pieces and put them on a cookie sheet. The children watched with enthusiasm as she did these last few steps.

While the kids were watching what Ms. Whisk was doing, they had not noticed that the room was changing!

Cardboard boxes cut themselves into pieces to turn into the Pyramid of Giza. The circle time carpet turned into the Nile River. The classroom cabinets turned into a long stretch of desert. Ribbons and curtains came off the walls to make Egyptian-style fashion for everyone.

The chalk started to write hieroglyphics on the board. The chalk also wrote, "Welcome to Egypt!" in the Egyptian alphabet.

The children were all so amazed at what was happening that they jumped in and started to make headdresses and necklaces by cutting paper into a variety of shapes and then gluing them together.

Ms. Whisk looked at what was happening and knew that the children were engaged in great learning. It warmed her heart to see all the excitement. She knew that the children were going to start asking questions about Egypt once the magic started and things changed.

She said, "Learn from this magic that was created by you!"

Baklava

Total time
30 minutes
Makes 4
servings

Ingredients

1 cup (240ml) chopped nuts, any kind

1 cup (240ml) flaked coconut

3 tablespoons (45ml) softened butter

1 box phyllo dough*

Nonstick cooking spray (butter-flavor)

Nonstick cooking spray original

1 cup (240ml) sugar

1 cup (240ml) water

1 teaspoon (5ml) lemon juice

½ (2.5ml) vanilla sugar (recipe follows)

1 teaspoon (5ml) butter

*Most grocery stores carry Phyllo dough (Athens brand)

*vanilla sugar recipe: 2 cups granulated sugar

1 teaspoon pure Vanilla Extract

Equipment

Mixing spoon, measuring cup, medium sized bowl, wax paper, paper towels, large cutting board, sharp knife, baking sheet, small saucepan, measuring spoons, whisk, wire rack, shallow baking pan, metal spatula

FOR MORE RECIPES, VISIT
COOLINARYCORNER.COM

DIRECTIONS

Preheat oven to 300 degrees F (150c). Take the spoon to mix the chopped nuts and flaked coconut together in a bowl. Add the softened butter and mix well. Take the phyllo dough out of the box, carefully unroll the sheets, and lay them flat on your work surface. Phyllo dries out quickly, so place a sheet of waxed paper over the phyllo and cover with a damp paper towels. Take 1 phyllo sheet and lay it on a large cutting board. Phyllo can tear easily so be gentle (the first few sheets may tear, put them aside and use the first sheet that peels off without tearing) Lightly spray the entire surface of the first phyllo sheet with the butter-flavored cooking spray. Continue laying seven more sheets of phyllo on top of the first spraying each one with the butter-flavored cooking spray as you lay it down. Finally, spray the last, top sheet. Spread the nut and coconut mixture in a line along one of the edges of the phyllo. Lightly spray the mixture with the butter-flavored cooking spray. Starting at that edge, carefully roll the phyllo until you get to the other edge. It will look like a thick log. Lightly spray the log, especially the seam, with the butter-flavored cooking spray. Slice the phyllo log at an angle, dividing it into sections. Spray the baking sheet with the original cooking spray. Place the pieces of baklava on the baking sheet and bake for about 35 minutes or until lightly browned. While the pieces are baking, make the "honey" syrup. Put the sugar, water, and lemon juice in the saucepan, whisk to blend, and bring to a boil on high heat, then turn down the heat to medium and simmer until the syrup thickens about 20 minutes. Stir occasionally. Add the vanilla sugar and the butter and stir until the butter is melted. Turn off the heat and set the syrup aside. Place the rack in the baking pan, then use the spatula to carefully place the pieces of baklava on the rack to cool completely. Pour the honey over the cooled baklava pieces. Let the syrup drip off into the baking pan. Don't throw away the syrup that drips into the baking pan. Save it to drizzle over the leftover pieces of baklava the next day.

ENJOY!

VANILLA SUGAR RECIPE

Place sugar in a large ziplock bag. Add vanilla. Seal bag. Knead sugar until the vanilla is evenly distributed. Spread sugar on rimmed baking sheet. Let stand 25 to 30 minutes or until sugar is dried. Store in airtight container. If sugar clumps up, break apart by rubbing between fingers.

ABOUT THE ILLUSTRATOR

MOLLY MCGREEVY lives in Miami FL. Her two most favorite things in this world are cutting fun shapes out of colored paper and making chocolate chip cookies with her two children, Lillian and Nate. They can't wait to try out the baklava recipe in this book. You can find out more about her artwork and writings at mollymcgreevy.com.

CPSIA information can be obtained
at www.ICGtesting.com
Printed in the USA
LVHW06*0455070418
572614LV00001B/1/P